World War II in Europe

Kelly Rodgers

Consultant

Jennifer M. Lopez, NBCT, M.S.Ed.
Teacher Specialist—History/Social Studies
Office of Curriculum & Instruction
Norfolk Public Schools

Publishing Credits

Rachelle Cracchiolo, M.S.Ed., *Publisher*
Conni Medina, M.A.Ed., *Managing Editor*
Emily R. Smith, M.A.Ed., *Content Director*
Véronique Bos, *Creative Director*
Robin Erickson, *Art Director*
Michelle Jovin, M.A., *Associate Editor*
Fabiola Sepulveda, *Graphic Designer*

Image Credits: front cover, p.1, p.7 (bottom), p.10, p.17 (bottom) Everett Historical/Shutterstock; pp.2–3 U.S. Air Force; pp.4–5 World History Archive/Alamy; p.6 (left) 360b/Shutterstock; p.6 (right) Three Lions/Getty Images; p.7 (top) FDR Presidential Library & Museum; p.8 Corbis via Getty Images; p.9 (top) TCM; p.9 (left), p.14 (top), p.24 (top), p.25 (left), p.26, p.27, p.28 (bottom right) U.S National Archives; p.9 (right) Wellcome Library; p.11 Central Press/Hulton Archive/Getty Images; p.12 Library of Congress [LC-DIG-ppmsca-12898]; p.13 (top) Pictorial Press Ltd/Alamy; p.13 (bottom) National Museum of the U.S. Navy; p.14 (bottom) U.S. Naval History and Heritage Command; p15 (top) LOC [LC-USW33-000138-ZE]; p.15 (bottom) LOC [LC-DIG-ppmsca-13260]; p.16 (left) LOC [LC-USZC4-4435]; p.16 (right) Linda Steward/iStock; p.17 (top) LOC [LC-DIG-fsac-1a35369]; p.17 (top) LOC [LC-DIG-fsac-1a35369]; p.18 (top) LOC [LC-DIG-fsa-8d29114]; p.18 (bottom) LOC [LC-DIG-fsa-8d29109]; p.19 (top) San Jose State University Department of Special Collections and Archive; p.19 (bottom) Everett Collection Historical/Alamy; pp.20–21 Russian International News Agency; p.21 (right) U.S. Navy; p.22 U.S. Army; p. 23 (bottom) World History Archive/Alamy; p.24 (bottom) German Federal Archives; p.25 (right) United States Holocaust Memorial Museum, courtesy of Belarusian State Archive of Documentary Film and Photography; p.28 (bottom left) Churchill Archives Centre; p.29 Imperial War Museum; p.32 U.S. Coast Guard, photo by Chief Photographer's Mate Robert F. Sargent; all other images from iStock and/or Shutterstock.

Library of Congress Cataloging-in-Publication Data

Names: Rodgers, Kelly, author.
Title: World War II in Europe / Kelly Rodgers.
Other titles: World War 2 in Europe
Description: Huntington Beach, CA : Teacher Created Materials, [2020] | Summary: "World War II was the bloodiest, most destructive war in history. The European Theater played host to some of the most significant events of the war. When the war drew to a close in 1945, more than 40 million people were dead. Cities lay in ruins. Millions of people were homeless. It would take decades for Europe to recover from the devastation."-- Provided by publisher.
Identifiers: LCCN 2019024372 (print) | LCCN 2019024373 (ebook) | ISBN 9781425850708 (paperback) | ISBN 9781425850708 (ebook)
Subjects: LCSH: World War, 1939-1945--Europe--Juvenile literature. | World War, 1939-1945--United States--Juvenile literature. | Holocaust, Jewish (1939-1945)--Juvenile literature.
Classification: LCC D756.3 .R63 2020 (print) | LCC D756.3 (ebook) | DDC 940.53/4--dc23
LC record available at https://lccn.loc.gov/2019024372

TCM Teacher Created Materials
5301 Oceanus Drive
Huntington Beach, CA 92649-1030
www.tcmpub.com
ISBN 978-1-4258-5070-8

Printed by: 51497
Printed in: China

Table of Contents

The World at War 4

An Uneasy Peace 6

Europe Ignites 10

America Enters the War 14

On to Victory 20

The Holocaust 24

Legacy of Hope 26

Stage It! 28

Glossary 30

Index 31

Your Turn! 32

The World at War

World War II was one of the most important and devastating events of the twentieth century. More than 40 million people lost their lives. The war cost over $1 trillion. Cities were ruined. People around the world were affected.

At the same time, great progress was made. New technologies were invented. Medicines were created. Discoveries changed the lives of people all over the world. Important social changes arose during the war. Women, African Americans, and others were encouraged to join the work force—many for the first time. The Great Depression came to an end in most countries.

How could such a destructive event bring about so much good? What was it about the war that showcased the worst and the best in humanity?

World War II was a global war; nearly every country took part in it in some way. The war was fought between the Axis powers and the Allied forces. The Axis side included Germany, Italy, and Japan. The countries leading the Allies were Great Britain, the Soviet Union, and the United States. After six long years of fighting, the Allies won. When the war ended, people everywhere hoped peace would last.

The Slinky

In 1943, American engineer Richard James was working to solve a problem for U.S. naval ships. The navy needed a way to keep sensitive instruments from bouncing around in rough waters. While working, James bumped a box of tools off a shelf. A spring fell to the ground and seemed to walk. James and his wife took out a loan for $500 to develop their walking toy. His wife came up with the name—Slinky®.

Medical Marvels

Great medical advancements were made during World War II to treat wounded and sick soldiers. New medicines helped fight infections. **Skin grafting** was used for treating burn victims. The process for transferring blood from one person to another was perfected. New vaccines were introduced. In the middle of so much death, improvements in health care held great promise.

An Uneasy Peace

When World War I ended in 1918, an uneasy peace settled over the world. For a short time, people celebrated. But peace did not bring **stability**. The end of the war did not solve everything. The Treaty of Versailles of 1919 had ended the war. But the treaty set harsh terms for Germany. The German government had to pay to fix all damage to the Allied countries from the war. The terms wrecked Germany's economy. They were not alone. Many countries had spent a lot of money during the war. Now, they owed large **debts**. To add to the chaos, governments across Europe were becoming unstable. Revolutions and civil wars broke out.

The Price of Bread

Germany's economy was ruined after World War I. Before the war, a loaf of bread cost less than 1 **mark** (about $4 in 1913). After the war, German money had completely lost its value. That same loaf of bread cost 200 trillion marks (about $4 billion in 1923). The German government printed bills worth $10 billion marks each. Workers used laundry baskets and suitcases to carry their earnings home.

The People's Car

In 1934, the German government was trying to fix its economy. They thought building a new roadway would help. They called it the *autobahn*. To promote travel, they created *Volkswagen*, or the "People's Car." Their cars sold for $140 each (around $2,000 today). This brand of car is still sold.

▼ German marks became so worthless that some children used them as toys.

Then, in 1929, the Great Depression began. During this time, millions of people lost their jobs. People were homeless and starving. These people looked to their governments for help. In the United States, Americans elected President Franklin D. Roosevelt in 1932. He set to work right away and started new programs to create jobs and help people. Elsewhere, **nationalist** leaders rose to power in parts of Europe and Japan. They promised a better future for their citizens. Instead, their actions would soon lead to a second world war.

▼ President Roosevelt

▼ Many homeless people lived in settlements like this during the Great Depression.

Threatening Dictators

Nationalist leaders were making sweeping changes. The Soviet leader, Joseph Stalin, said only the government could own businesses and land. In Italy, Prime Minister Benito Mussolini got rid of free press. Both Mussolini and Stalin stressed the good of the nation over the good of the people.

In the early 1930s, Adolf Hitler was rising to power in Germany. In 1934, Hitler became president of Germany. His **Nazi** Party worked to build an empire called the Third Reich (RIKE). Hitler hoped to create a **master race**. He planned to take over more land so Germans could live and thrive.

In 1936, Hitler made his first move. He sent German soldiers to an area of land on the French border called the Rhineland. After World War I, German leaders had agreed to remove all military forces from the Rhineland. Hitler's move broke that agreement. Two years later, German troops took control of Austria. Still, Hitler was not satisfied. He wanted more land and more power. French and British leaders grew worried. Hitler asked them to meet with him in Munich. There, Hitler said that he was uniting the German people. He told them he only wanted one more piece of land and then he would stop. The leaders believed him. So, they made a deal called the Munich Agreement. The **pact** gave part of Czechoslovakia to Germany.

British, French, German, and Italian leaders at the signing of the Munich Agreement

Germany's Movements 1936–1938

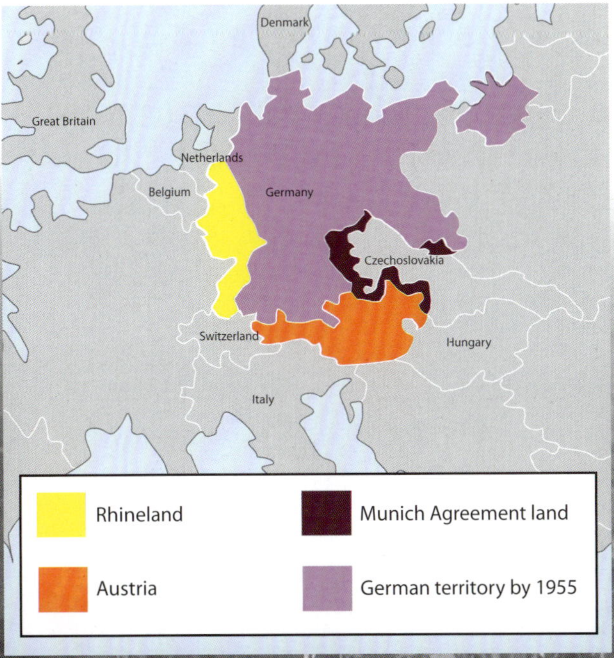

Hitler salutes his troops in November 1935.

The Berlin Olympics

In August 1936, the Olympic Games® took place in Berlin. Due to Hitler's racist views, only one non-**Aryan** athlete was put on the German team. African American athlete Jesse Owens struck gold for the U.S. team. He won four track-and-field events. He was proof that Hitler's prejudiced beliefs were false.

Chamberlain's Error

British Prime Minister Neville Chamberlain (shown above) was one of the leaders who met with Hitler in Munich. When Chamberlain returned home, he told the British people that there would be peace, not war. He thought giving Hitler what he wanted would be enough.

Europe Ignites

Hitler had succeeded in his plan to unite the Germanic people of Europe. Yet he still wanted more land and power. Hitler set out to take both.

Blitzkrieg

On September 1, 1939, German forces invaded Poland. British and French leaders declared war on Germany two days later. There was no turning back. German troops had a new strategy for taking over Europe called *blitzkrieg* (BLITS-kreeg), or "lightning war." World War I had been fought largely in the **trenches**. With blitzkrieg, German forces moved quickly and struck at the enemy with heavy firepower. It proved to be very successful. Within a year, the German Army controlled much of Europe, including France.

A German bomber plane flies over London during the Blitz.

Underground

Winston Churchill became Great Britain's prime minister on May 10, 1940. When the Blitz began, he and his advisors moved to an underground **bunker** for the rest of the war. They had maps, food, and a phone line to President Roosevelt. They stayed underground for days or weeks at a time. Each time they came to the surface, they saw just how much damage the Blitz was causing.

Dunkirk

As German troops stormed across France, British officer John Vereker **retreated** to the French port of Dunkirk. A call went out across England for all boats to make their way to the port to help. Fishing boats, ferries, and motorboats flooded into Dunkirk. Over the next few days, 338,000 Allied troops were rescued. These men were able to continue the fight against the Axis powers.

Battle of Britain

Hitler set his sights on Great Britain next. To be successful, Hitler had to fight a new type of war from the air. From July 10 to October 31, 1940, German planes attacked nonstop in a move known as the Blitz. The British Royal Air Force kept the country safe from a German invasion. They were helped by a new technology called *radar*. It allowed the British to track German planes, even in the dark. Great Britain stood strong. But to fight back, they would need help from their ally across the ocean.

▼ **This building was destroyed during the Blitz.**

American Neutrality

Great Britain wanted the United States to enter the war. However, during the 1930s, the U.S. Congress passed laws called the Neutrality Acts. These acts were meant to keep the country out of war. Some Americans believed that World War I was a mistake. They did not want to be drawn in to another war on a foreign continent. Still, Roosevelt knew he had to help the war effort in Europe.

In 1940, Roosevelt created new policies to send **aid** to countries fighting Hitler. In a program called Lend-Lease, the United States sent guns and ships to the British. Meanwhile, members of Congress knew the United States could not completely stay out of the war forever. So, they increased the amount of money that was spent on the military. They also began a **draft**—the first one during a time when the country was not actively at war.

Knowing that the nation was in danger, Roosevelt ran for a third term as president. Presidents serving only two terms was a long-standing tradition. Roosevelt broke the tradition because he felt it was not the right time for a change in leadership. Voters agreed and re-elected Roosevelt in 1940.

On June 22, 1941, Hitler attacked the Soviet Union. Stalin joined the Allies in their effort to defeat Hitler. Three months later, a British aircraft dropped a bomb near a German submarine. The Germans believed a U.S. ship, the USS *Greer*, was responsible for the bomb. They fired upon the U.S. ship. After that, Roosevelt ordered the navy to shoot German submarines on sight.

▲ German troops invade the Soviet Union.

The Arsenal of Democracy

When Roosevelt was elected, he began addressing the nation over the radio. He called these speeches "fireside chats." In 1940, Roosevelt gave one of these chats. Even though Americans were not fighting, he said they played an important role. He said they had to help defeat Hitler. In that speech, he said, "We must be the great **arsenal** of democracy. For us, this is an emergency as serious as war itself."

▼ USS *Greer*

Switching Sides

Before the war started, Stalin tried to get Great Britain and France to stand up to Hitler. However, British and French leaders thought war could be avoided. So, Stalin joined Hitler instead. For two years, the Soviet Union fought with the Axis side. Hitler's 1941 invasion caused the Soviet Union to switch sides and join the Allies.

America Enters the War

On December 7, 1941, Japanese planes bombed the Pearl Harbor naval base in Hawai'i. Thousands of people were killed or wounded. People were stunned. The next day, Congress declared war against Japan. On December 11, the Axis powers responded by declaring war on the United States. That same day, the United States declared war on all Axis powers. The United States had finally joined the war.

Women in Service

In August 1943, the Women Airforce Service Pilots (WASP) was formed. More than 25,000 women applied to the program. Less than 10 percent were accepted. Those who were chosen had to go through an intense training program. By the end of the war, the women of WASP had flown more than 60 million miles (100 million kilometers).

A Duck Gets Drafted

During the war, Walt Disney and others created cartoons to keep Americans supporting the war effort. Disney's most famous wartime cartoon was called *Der Fuehrer's Face*. In it, Donald Duck® has a dream that he is forced to work in a Nazi factory making weapons. At the end of the episode, Donald wakes up. The final scene is a tomato hitting Hitler in the face.

▼ This photograph was taken from a Japanese plane during the attack on Pearl Harbor.

▲ Americans sign up to join the military in January 1942.

▲ Tuskegee Airmen receive instructions for their next mission.

The draft had been in place for over a year. Still, the United States needed more soldiers. So, Congress passed laws that let women serve in **noncombat** roles. Hundreds of thousands of women answered the call. Millions of men volunteered to join the armed forces too.

African American pilots trained at an air base in Tuskegee, Alabama. The men there fought for the "Double V Campaign." The two Vs stood for *victory* over America's enemies in the war and *victory* over racism at home. Many Tuskegee Airmen won awards for their courage in battle. These men paved the way for the civil rights movement 20 years later. But for now, the Allies needed more than just soldiers to win the war.

How the Nation Responded

As soldiers fought overseas, they relied on help from the home front. The *home front* describes nonsoldiers who help in a war effort. Work on the home front often makes the difference between winning and losing a war.

From cars to food, American factories helped win the war. People in car factories built jeeps, tanks, and planes. In soda factories, workers filled bottles with explosives instead of drinks. Factory owners needed help to fill the gaps from the men who left to fight in the war. Those people who had been denied jobs in the past, including women and racial minorities, were now in demand. Some defense plants ran 24-hour day cares, which allowed mothers to work at all times of day and night.

There was a war to be won. Every man, woman, and child knew they had a role to play. Prices on goods were frozen and taxes were raised. **War bonds** were sold to raise more money. The government distributed **ration books**. Under this system, Americans could only buy small amounts of certain things. These restricted items included gasoline, coffee, sugar, and meat. Families planted "victory gardens" and grew their own food. People tried to help in any way they could.

▲ ad for war bonds

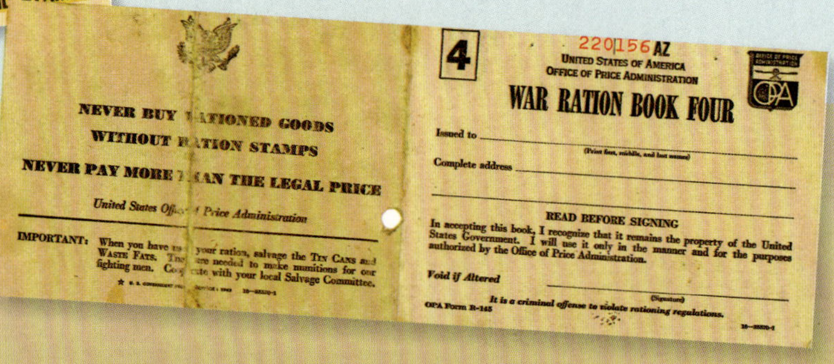

ration book ▶

▲ This woman works in a factory assembling war planes in 1943.

▲ Factory workers assemble bomber planes.

Rosie the Riveter

In 1942, a song called "Rosie the Riveter" was released. The lyrics tell of a girl named Rosie who is "making history, working for victory." Rosie helped change public opinion about women joining the workforce. One year after the song was released, artist Norman Rockwell drew his version of Rosie. Rockwell's Rosie wore a work jumpsuit and had a copy of Hitler's book, *Mein Kampf*, under her feet.

Young Collectors

During the war, children collected recyclables to help the war effort. Foil wrappers from chocolate bars were used to confuse radar systems. Old toothpaste tubes were turned into weapons. And cooking fat was made into explosives.

Tax Facts

The Sixteenth Amendment to the U.S. Constitution was passed in 1913. It charged a tax on what people earned in their jobs. Before World War I, the top rate someone paid to the government was 7 percent of their total income. Due to tax increases during World War II, that number jumped to 94 percent!

Braceros Today

American farmers started to depend on foreign labor. After the war, the Bracero Program was replaced with the H-2 Program. This program allows foreign-born people to enter the United States to find work. Today, foreign-born workers make up 78 percent of all U.S. farmworkers. They also make up 16 percent of the rest of the workforce.

The war took millions of men away from their jobs including those men who worked on farms. But Americans at home and troops overseas still needed food. To help with labor shortages on farms, Mexican workers were asked to come to the United States. These workers were called *braceros*. They provided a much-needed service during the war. This was meant to be a temporary act. However, American farmers came to rely on Mexican labor.

▲ Braceros arrive in Stockton, California.

Braceros harvest sugar beets in 1943. ▼

At the same time, there was prejudice and fear. Minority workers often faced racism. In California, violence broke out between Mexican American workers and U.S. sailors. The **riots** lasted for six days. Military police had to step in and take control.

After the attack on Pearl Harbor, Japanese Americans were targeted. On Roosevelt's order, around 125,000 Japanese Americans on the West Coast were forced into **internment camps**. These people had to give up their homes and jobs. Life in the camps was difficult. It was common for around 25 people to share a room that was meant for 4 people. They were under the constant watch of armed guards. They lived behind barbed-wire fences. Their lives would never be the same.

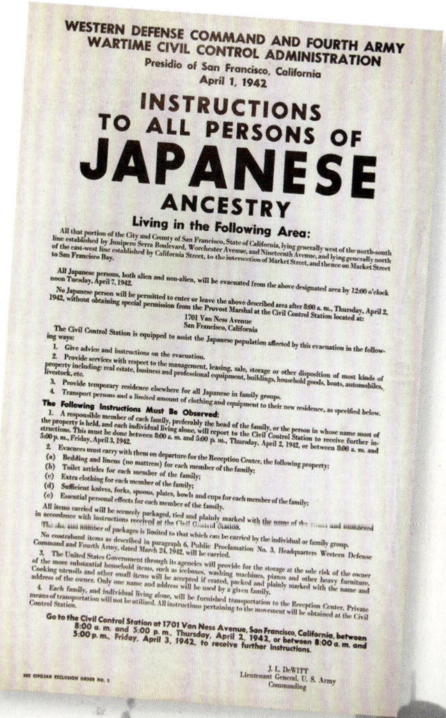

WESTERN DEFENSE COMMAND AND FOURTH ARMY
WARTIME CIVIL CONTROL ADMINISTRATION
Presidio of San Francisco, California
April 1, 1942

INSTRUCTIONS
TO ALL PERSONS OF
JAPANESE
ANCESTRY

Living in the Following Area:

All that portion of the City and County of San Francisco, State of California, lying generally west of the north-south line established by Junipero Serra Boulevard, Worchester Avenue, and Nineteenth Avenue, and lying generally north of the east-west line established by California Street, to the intersection of Market Street, and thence on Market Street to San Francisco Bay.

All Japanese persons, both alien and non-alien, will be evacuated from the above designated area by 12:00 o'clock noon Tuesday, April 7, 1942.

No Japanese person will be permitted to enter or leave the above described area after 8:00 a. m., Thursday, April 2, 1942, without obtaining special permission from the Provost Marshal at the Civil Control Station located at:

1701 Van Ness Avenue
San Francisco, California

The Civil Control Station is equipped to assist the Japanese population affected by this evacuation in the following ways:

1. Give advice and instructions on the evacuation.
2. Provide services with respect to the management, leasing, sale, storage or other disposition of most kinds of property including: real estate, business and professional equipment, buildings, household goods, boats, automobiles, livestock, etc.
3. Provide temporary residence elsewhere for all Japanese in family groups.
4. Transport persons and a limited amount of clothing and equipment to their new residence, as specified below.

The Following Instructions Must Be Observed:

1. A responsible member of each family, preferably the head of the family, or the person in whose name most of the property is held, and each individual living alone, will report to the Civil Control Station to receive further instructions. This must be done between 8:00 a. m. and 5:00 p. m., Thursday, April 2, 1942, or between 8:00 a. m. and 5:00 p. m., Friday, April 3, 1942.

2. Evacuees must carry with them on departure for the Reception Center, the following property:
(a) Bedding and linens (no mattress) for each member of the family;
(b) Toilet articles for each member of the family;
(c) Extra clothing for each member of the family;
(d) Sufficient knives, forks, spoons, plates, bowls and cups for each member of the family;
(e) Essential personal effects for each member of the family.

All items carried will be securely packaged, tied and plainly marked with the name of the [illegible] and numbered in accordance with instructions received at the Civil Control Station.

The [illegible] and number of packages is limited to that which can be carried by the individual or family group.

No contraband items as described in paragraph 6, Public Proclamation No. 3, Headquarters Western Defense Command and Fourth Army, dated March 24, 1942, will be carried.

3. The United States Government through its agencies will provide for the storage at the sole risk of the owner of the more substantial household items, such as iceboxes, washing machines, pianos and other heavy furniture. Cooking utensils and other small items will be accepted if crated, packed and plainly marked with the name and address of the owner. Only one name and address will be used by a given family.

4. Each family, and individual living alone, will be furnished transportation to the Reception Center. Private means of transportation will not be utilized. All instructions pertaining to the movement will be obtained at the Civil Control Station.

Go to the Civil Control Station at 1701 Van Ness Avenue, San Francisco, California, between 8:00 a. m. and 5:00 p. m., Thursday, April 2, 1942, or between 8:00 a. m. and 5:00 p. m., Friday, April 3, 1942, to receive further instructions.

J. L. DeWITT
Lieutenant General, U. S. Army
Commanding

SEE CIVILIAN EXCLUSION ORDER NO. 5

This poster notifies people of the plan to move them to internment camps. ▶

▼ People in internment camps stand behind barbed wire and wave to a passing train.

On to Victory

Overseas in Europe, the Allied forces were on the offensive. On November 8, 1942, they entered French North Africa. Six months of fierce fighting resulted in a win for the Allies. Next, they turned to Italy. With the help of the Tuskegee Airmen, the Allies took control there too.

Meanwhile, Germany progressed through the Soviet Union. The Battle of Stalingrad raged into the new year. It lasted six months and was the war's deadliest battle. The Soviets suffered 1,000,000 **casualties**; the Axis powers had 800,000. Even though they lost fewer men, it was the Germans who surrendered. They hoped to escape the harsh Soviet winter. This surrender proved to be the turning point of the war.

▼ **Soviet soldiers advance in the Battle of Stalingrad.**

Next, the Allies planned Operation Overlord. It would later be known as D-Day. On June 6, 1944, more than 160,000 Allied soldiers stormed five beaches in Normandy, France. With them came thousands of ships and planes. A long, bloody battle against German forces followed. After a month of fighting, there were more than 500,000 casualties. In the end, the Allies won. Now, they were ready to push through and free the rest of Europe. France, Belgium, and Luxembourg were free by September. It was time for the Allies to turn their attention to Germany.

London Blackout

On August 11, 1939, London went dark. Outside lights turned off and blackout curtains drew closed. The British government had ordered the blackout, having correctly guessed that the nation would be a target for German bombings. The blackout later spread to all the United Kingdom and was in effect until September 1944. As the government became more confident in their win, they lessoned the restrictions to a so-called "dim-out." All restrictions on lighting were removed by April 1945.

Kid Vet

To serve in the U.S. armed forces, people must be at least 17 years old. Calvin Graham lied about his age—he was only 12—and joined the U.S. Navy. He also lied to his mother. Graham said he was going to visit relatives. Graham served on the USS *South Dakota* and saw some of the most brutal fighting of the war. He was injured and earned a Purple Heart—a medal given to soldiers who are wounded or killed while serving.

The Battle of the Bulge

In December 1944, Hitler's troops made one last attempt to win the war. Faced with a likely defeat, they turned back to their former blitzkrieg tactics. They wedged into the center of the Allied battle line. The front line of fighting took on a bulging appearance. Hitler hoped to split the Allied forces in two. However, the Allies stayed strong and held their position. American forces attacked the sides of the German forces. The German troops were forced to retreat. The last German soldiers withdrew on January 16, 1945, as the Allies won the battle. Now, there was little to stand in the way of an Allied victory in the war in Europe.

▲ U.S. soldiers take cover during the Battle of the Bulge.

A Future Queen's War Effort

When England's Princess Elizabeth was 18 years old, she made a bold move. She joined the Women's Auxiliary Territorial Service. That was the women's branch of the British Army. She worked as both a mechanic and a truck driver during the war. Within a decade of the end of the war, she would be crowned queen of England.

Cracking the Code

Colossus, built in 1943, was one of the world's earliest digital computers. It took up an entire room and was made from 1,700 vacuum tubes. Colossus was used in Project Ultra, which cracked the Axis powers' secret codes. By cracking the codes, the Allies knew where the Axis troops would be located. Code breaking was key to winning the war.

Victory in Europe

Allied troops next pushed their way into Berlin. They hoped to capture the German leaders. However, before they could reach Hitler, he killed himself in an underground bunker. The next week, Germany surrendered. At midnight on May 8, 1945, the war in Europe was finally over. The full horror of Nazi rule was exposed for the world to see.

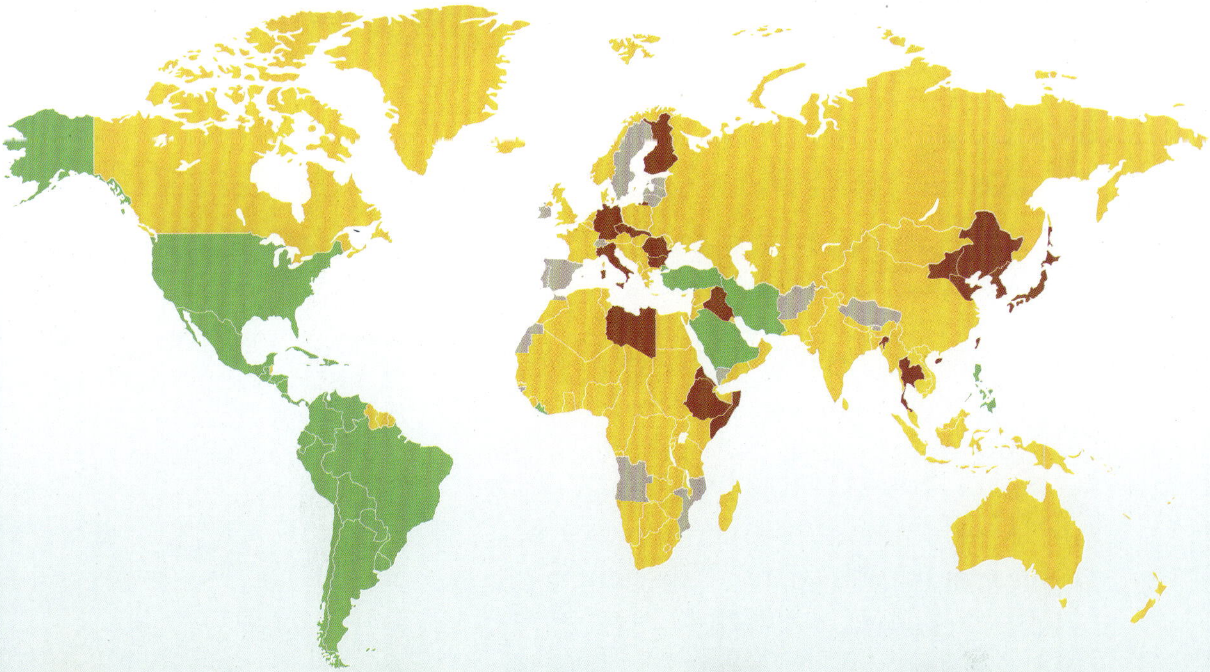

Allied countries before the Japanese attack on Pearl Harbor

Allied countries that entered the war after the attack on Pearl Harbor

Axis powers

neutral countries

A crowd in London celebrates V-E Day—Victory in Europe Day.

The Holocaust

Allied troops making their way across Europe made a grim discovery—**concentration camps**. Six million Jewish men, women, and children had been cruelly murdered. Millions of other non-Jewish people met the same fate. This campaign of terror is known as the Holocaust. Part of Hitler's plan had been taking over land to make room for people he thought were worth more. This included blond, blue-eyed Aryans. He and his followers murdered millions of people to make that vision a reality.

▲ Survivors at a concentration camp lie in their beds.

New prisoners arrive at the Auschwitz concentration camp in the summer of 1944.

On January 27, 1945, Allied soldiers arrived at Auschwitz, Poland. It was the site of the camp with the highest death toll. Allied troops saw thousands of sick and starving victims. They also discovered millions of items of clothing. They found thousands of pounds of human hair.

Over the next year, war crime trials were held in Germany. Hitler was dead, but other Nazi leaders were held responsible for the Holocaust. Judges from the Allied countries oversaw 22 trials. Some people were sentenced to death. Others had to serve time in prison. The trials showed that even leaders could be punished for crimes against humanity.

▲ World leaders watch the sentencing of war criminals responsible for the Holocaust during the Nuremberg Trials.

We Are Free!

Eva Mozes Kor was 10 years old when the Allies came to get her out of Auschwitz. She remembered a woman running through the camp yelling that they were free. Kor went outside, and through the snow, she could see Allied troops coming into the camp. She and the other prisoners ran to the soldiers. "They gave us chocolates, cookies, and hugs. And this was my first taste of freedom," Kor said.

Survivor

Elie Wiesel was 15 years old when he and his family were sent to concentration camps. Wiesel's mother, father, and sister all died in the Holocaust. When the Allies opened the camps, Wiesel was freed. He moved to the United States. He worked as an author and a professor. Wiesel was awarded the Nobel Peace Prize in 1986. When he accepted the award, he said, "Human suffering anywhere concerns men and women everywhere."

Legacy of Hope

A New President

Harry S. Truman was vice president for only 82 days. That's when Roosevelt died, and Truman became president. Truman's first months in office were filled with challenges. The United States was still fighting Japan in World War II's Pacific Theater. Many people around the world were suffering. It was Truman's job to help steer the country out of the war and into a more peaceful future.

Finding a Home

As war drew to a close in Europe, it is believed that around 21 million people were refugees. *Refugees* are people who have been forced to flee their homelands in a crisis. More than half of those people had been forced to do hard labor. By 1951, there were still one million refugees without homes.

As peace returned to Europe, people paused to reflect on the past six years. The war brought many changes. Women and minorities had new opportunities in the United States. Old prejudices were being examined. The economy of the United States was booming. But all this social change had come at a terrible cost. Millions of people had died in the war. Nations lay in ruins. How had the world been consumed by war again so quickly? Was there something that could be done to prevent such devastation in the future?

On May 8, 1945, the Allies had celebrated V-E Day, victory in Europe. Sadly, President Roosevelt did not live to see it. He had died one month earlier, on April 12. Before Roosevelt died, he began working on a plan for peace, a legacy of hope. The plan called for a group of representatives from around the world to help keep peace—this organization was to be called the United Nations. The United Nations still exists.

Since the end of World War II, there have been no major world wars. This time has been called the "Long Peace." A legacy of hope for a more peaceful world continues.

After her husband's death, Eleanor Roosevelt helped make the United Nations a reality. ▲

Americans celebrate V-J Day—Victory over Japan Day—on September 2, 1945.

STAGE IT!

The wartime speeches of President Roosevelt and Prime Minister Churchill were important weapons for the Allies. Their words encouraged American and British soldiers to keep fighting and win the war.

Find some of Roosevelt's and Churchill's speeches online. Listen to a few recordings. Think about what people might have been feeling as they heard these words. How might people have reacted to their leaders in this time of crisis? Were they nervous, or did their leaders give them confidence? Then, choose one speech that you find the most impactful. Write and perform a skit as if you were listening to these words for the first time during the war.

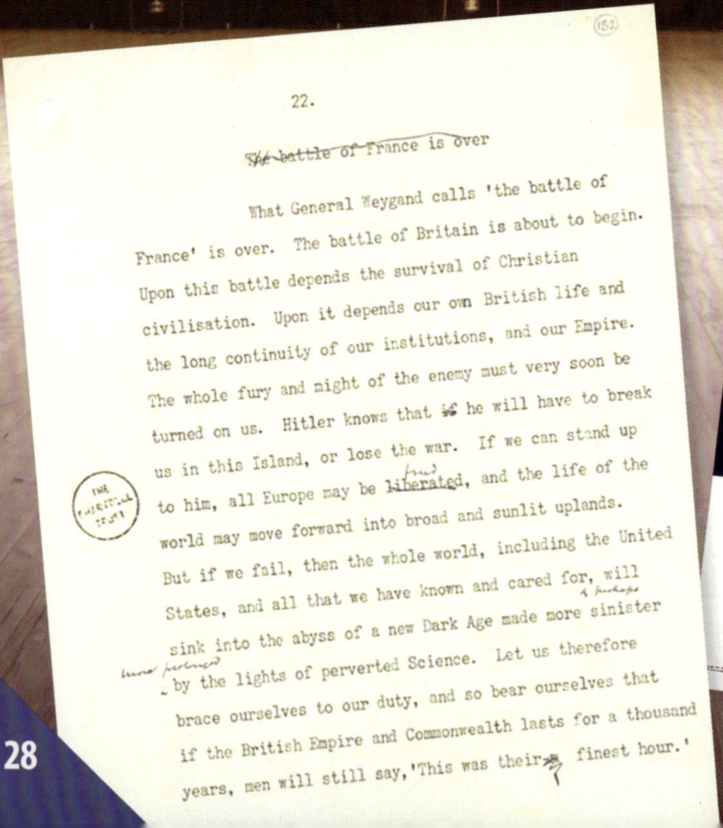
22.

The battle of France is over

What General Weygand calls 'the battle of France' is over. The battle of Britain is about to begin. Upon this battle depends the survival of Christian civilisation. Upon it depends our own British life and the long continuity of our institutions, and our Empire. The whole fury and might of the enemy must very soon be turned on us. Hitler knows that he will have to break us in this Island, or lose the war. If we can stand up to him, all Europe may be liberated, and the life of the world may move forward into broad and sunlit uplands. But if we fail, then the whole world, including the United States, and all that we have known and cared for, will sink into the abyss of a new Dark Age made more sinister by the lights of perverted Science. Let us therefore brace ourselves to our duty, and so bear ourselves that if the British Empire and Commonwealth lasts for a thousand years, men will still say, 'This was their finest hour.'

G LTD

Glossary

aid—help or assistance

arsenal—a place for collecting or manufacturing something

Aryan—term used in Nazism to refer to non-Jewish Caucasians

bunker—a shelter that is dug into the ground to protect someone from attack

casualties—people who are killed, captured, or seriously injured during warfare

concentration camps—prisons where civilians are kept during wars

debts—money owed to others

draft—a selection of people from the general population for military service

internment camps—prisons where people are kept for political reasons during wars

mark—an old form of German money

master race—people believed by Nazis to be racially superior and fit to rule others

nationalist—refers to people who think their countries are superior to other countries

Nazi—German political party, ruled by Adolf Hitler, which controlled the country from 1933 to 1945

noncombat—not actively fighting, especially in a war

pact—a formal agreement between two countries or groups, especially to agree to stop fighting

ration books—books that tell people how much food or supplies they are allowed per day

retreated—moved away from the threat of danger or attack

riots—public disturbances

skin grafting—a medical procedure that involves removing skin from one area of the body and moving it to a damaged part of the body

stability—the state of something that is not likely to change

trenches—ditches dug into the ground that can be used to protect soldiers

war bonds—government investments sold to raise money for war efforts

Index

Battle of Britain, 11

Battle of Stalingrad, 20

Battle of the Bulge, 22

Blitz, 10–11

blitzkrieg, 10, 22

braceros, 18

British Royal Air Force, 11

Chamberlain, Neville, 9

Churchill, Winston, 10

Colossus, 22

D-Day, 21

Double V Campaign, 15

Dunkirk, 10

Graham, Calvin, 21

Great Depression, 4, 7

Hitler, Adolf, 8–14, 17, 22, 24–25

Holocaust, 24–25

home front, 16–17

Lend-Lease, 12

Munich Agreement, 8

Mussolini, Benito, 8

Nazi, 8, 14, 22, 25

Neutrality Acts, 12

Olympic Games, 9

Operation Overlord, 21

Owens, Jesse, 9

Pearl Harbor, 14, 19, 23

Roosevelt, Eleanor, 26

Roosevelt, Franklin D., 7, 10, 12–13, 19, 26

Rosie the Riveter, 17

Stalin, Joseph, 8, 12–13

Third Reich, 8

Truman, Harry S., 26

Tuskegee Airmen, 15, 20

United Nations, 26

USS *Greer*, 12–13

V-E Day, 23, 26

V-J Day, 27

Women Airforce Service Pilots (WASP), 14

World War I, 6, 8, 10, 12, 18

Your Turn!

Operation Overlord was the Allied invasion of western Europe. It began on June 6, 1944, which is often called D-Day. The invasion had been carefully planned for over a year. At 6:30 a.m., British, Canadian, and U.S. soldiers landed on five beaches in Normandy, France. They were met with fierce resistance from German soldiers. Slowly, Allied soldiers made their way farther inland. By the end of August, all of northern France was free from Axis control.

This photograph was taken by Robert F. Sargent at 7:40 a.m. on D-Day. It is called *Into the Jaws of Death* and shows U.S. soldiers leaving a coast guard boat to invade Omaha Beach. In the background, clouds and smoke waft over the beach. Write a poem about how this photograph makes you feel.